John Greenleaf Whittier

Mabel Martin

A Harvest Idyl

John Greenleaf Whittier

Mabel Martin
A Harvest Idyl

ISBN/EAN: 9783744664356

Printed in Europe, USA, Canada, Australia, Japan

Cover: Foto ©Thomas Meinert / pixelio.de

More available books at **www.hansebooks.com**

MABEL MARTIN

A HARVEST IDYL

BY

JOHN GREENLEAF WHITTIER

WITH ILLUSTRATIONS

BOSTON
JAMES R. OSGOOD AND COMPANY
Late Ticknor & Fields, and Fields Osgood & Co.
1876

Copyright, 1874.
By JAMES R. OSGOOD & CO.

NOTE

THE substance of this poem, under the name of The Witch's Daughter, was published some years ago in the volume entitled "Home Ballads." For reproducing it in its present form with some additions to its original text, the author hopes to find an excuse in the beauty of the illustrations which the change has suggested.

ILLUSTRATIONS

[*The engravings are by* A. V. S. ANTHONY, *under whose supervision the book is prepared.*]

	ARTIST.	PAGE.
MABEL MARTIN	MARY A. HALLOCK	*Front.*
VIGNETTE	JOHN J. HARLEY .	*Title.*
VIGNETTES TO NOTE	" "	5
VIGNETTE	" "	6
HEAD-PIECE TO ILLUSTRATIONS . .	A. R. WAUD . . .	7
BORDER TO PROEM	MARY A. HALLOCK .	13
VIGNETTE	A. R. WAUD . . .	14
THE RIVER VALLEY (*Half-title to Part One*)	"	. . . 15
VIGNETTE	"	. . . 16
"Across the level tableland"	T. MORAN	17

Illustrations.

"On its brink
With roots half bare the pine-trees cling" . . T. MORAN . . 18

"Yon wind-scourged sand-dunes, cold and bleak" " . . 19

"Pass with me down the path that winds
Through birches to the open land" . . " . . 21

"The household ruin, century-old" . . . . " . . 22

"Sit with me while the westering day
Falls slantwise down the quiet vale" . . " . . 23

"Deer Island's pines" . . . . " . . 24

THE HUSKING (*Half title to Part Two*) . . . . A. R. WAUD . 25

VIGNETTE. . . . . " . 26

"The old swallow-haunted barns" . . MARY A. HALLOCK 27

"On Esek Harden's oaken floor
Lay the heaped ears of unhusked corn" . T. MORAN . . 28

"Thither came young men and maids" MARY A. HALLOCK 29

"How pleasantly the rising moon" . . . . T. MORAN . . 30

"And quaint old songs their fathers sung" MARY A. HALLOCK 31

"The red-ear" . . . . T. MORAN . . 32

THE WITCH'S DAUGHTER (*Half-title to Part Three*) A. R. WAUD . 33

VIGNETTE. . . . . " . 34

"Mabel Martin sat apart" . . . . . . MARY A. HALLOCK 35

Illustrations.

"Curious thousands thronged to see
　Her mother at the gallows-tree" . . . MARY A. HALLOCK　36

"Young Mabel from her mother's grave
　Crept to her desolate hearth-stone" . 　"　　　"　　39

"O, dreary broke the winter days" . . T. MORAN 40

"Indian Summer's airs of balm" . . . 　　"　　. . . . 41

"She saw the horseshoe's curvéd charm" MARY A. HALLOCK 42

"Who turned, in Salem's dreary jail,
　Her worn old Bible o'er and o'er" . 　"　　　"　　43

"Small leisure have the poor for grief" . 　"　　　"　　44

THE CHAMPION (*Half-title to Part Four*) . . A. R. WAUD . . . 45

VIGNETTE . . . . 　　"　　. . . 46

"But cruel eyes have found her out" . MARY A. HALLOCK 47

"Her sad eyes met the troubled gaze
　Of one" . . . . 　"　　　"　　48

"Let Goody Martin rest in peace" . . 　"　　　"　　50

"But one sly maiden spake aside" . . 　"　　　"　　51

TAIL-PIECE . . . . 　"　　　"　　52

IN THE SHADOW (*Half-title to Part Five*) . A. R. WAUD . . . 53

VIGNETTE . . . . 　　"　　. . . 54

"The nameless terrors of the wood" . . MARY A. HALLOCK 55

Illustrations.

"She leaned against the door"	MARY A. HALLOCK	57
"Through the willow-boughs below She saw the rippled waters shine"	" "	58
"Across the wooded space The harvest lights of Harden shone"	T. MORAN	59
"The prayer, begun in faith, Grew to a low, despairing cry"	MARY A. HALLOCK	60
"A shadow on the moonlight fell"	" "	62
THE BETROTHAL (*Half-title to Part Six*)	A. R. WAUD	63
VIGNETTE	"	64
"You know rough Esek Harden well"	MARY A. HALLOCK	65
"When she smiled, Upon his knees, a little child"	" "	66
"Her tears of grief were tears of joy"	" "	67
"He led her through his dewy fields"	" "	68
"Henceforth she stands no more alone"	" "	69
"O, pleasantly the harvest-moon"	T. MORAN	71
"And the wind whispered, 'It is well!'"	"	72

MABEL MARTIN

I CALL the old time back: I bring my lay
In tender memory of the summer day
When, where our native river lapsed away,

We dreamed it over, while the thrushes made
Songs of their own, and the great pine-trees laid
On warm noonlights the masses of their shade.

And *she* was with us, living o'er again
Her life in ours, despite of years and pain, —
The Autumn's brightness after latter rain.

Beautiful in her holy peace as one
Who stands, at evening, when the work is done,
Glorified in the setting of the sun!

Her memory makes our common landscape seem
Fairer than any of which painters dream;
Lights the brown hills and sings in every stream;

For she whose speech was always truth's pure gold
Heard, not unpleased, its simple legends told,
And loved with us the beautiful and old.

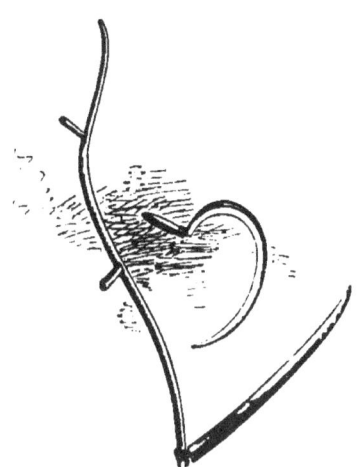

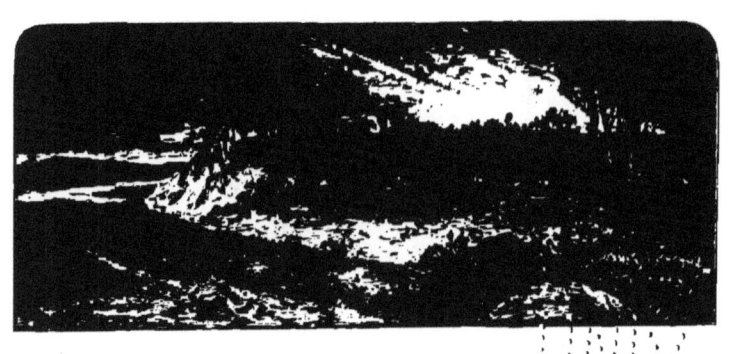

MABEL MARTIN.

Across the level tableland,

    A grassy, rarely trodden way,

    With thinnest skirt of birchen spray

And stunted growth of cedar, leads

    To where you see the dull plain fall

    Sheer off, steep-slanted, ploughed by all

PART I

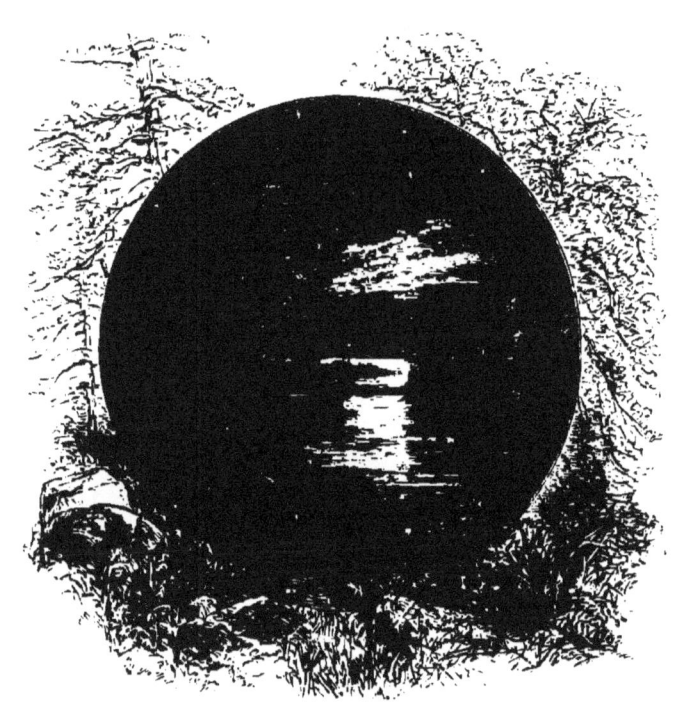

THE RIVER VALLEY

Mabel Martin.

The seasons' rainfalls. On its brink

The over-leaning harebells swing,

With roots half bare the pine-trees cling;

And, through the shadow

looking west,

You see the wavering

river flow

Along a vale, that far below

Mabel Martin.

Holds to the sun, the sheltering hills,

And glimmering water-line between,

Broad fields of corn and meadows green,

And fruit-bent orchards grouped around

The low brown roofs and painted eaves,

And chimney-tops half hid in leaves.

No warmer valley hides behind

Yon wind-scourged sand-dunes, cold and bleak;

No fairer river comes to seek

Mabel Martin.

The wave-sung welcome of the sea,

 Or mark the northmost border line

 Of sun-loved growths of nut and vine.

Here, ground-fast in their native fields,

 Untempted by the city's gain,

 The quiet farmer folk remain

Who bear the pleasant name of Friends,

 And keep their fathers' gentle ways

 And simple speech of Bible days;

In whose neat homesteads woman holds

 With modest ease her equal place,

 And wears upon her tranquil face

Mabel Martin.

The look of one who, merging not

Her self-hood in another's will,

Is love's and duty's handmaid still.

Pass with me down the path that winds

Through birches to the open land,

Where, close upon the river strand

Mabel Martin.

You mark a cellar, vine o'errun,

Above whose wall of loosened stones

The sumach lifts its reddening cones,

And the black nightshade's berries shine,

And broad, unsightly burdocks fold

The household ruin, century-old.

Mabel Martin.

Here, in the dim colonial time

    Of sterner lives and gloomier faith,

    A woman lived, tradition saith,

Who wrought her neighbors foul annoy,

    And witched and plagued the country-side,

    Till at the hangman's hand she died.

Sit with me while the westering day

    Falls slantwise down the quiet vale,

    And, haply, ere yon loitering sail,

Mabel Martin.

That rounds the upper headland, falls

  Below Deer Island's pines, or sees

  Behind it Hawkswood's belt of trees

Rise black against the sinking sun,

  My idyl of its days of old,

  The valley's legend shall be told.

PART II

THE HUSKING

It was the pleasant harvest-time,

When cellar-bins

are closely stowed,

And garrets bend

beneath their load,

And the old swallow-haunted barns, —

Brown-gabled, long, and full of seams

Through which the moted sunlight streams,

Mabel Martin.

And winds blow freshly in, to shake

    The red plumes of the roosted cocks,

    And the loose hay-mow's scented locks, —

Are filled with summer's ripened stores,

    Its odorous grass and barley sheaves,

    From their low scaffolds to their eaves.

On Esek Harden's oaken floor,

    With many an autumn threshing worn,

    Lay the heaped ears of unhusked corn.

Mabel Martin.

And thither came young men and maids,

Beneath a moon that, large and low,

Lit that sweet eve of long ago.

They took their places; some by chance,

And others by a merry voice

Or sweet smile guided to their choice.

Mabel Martin.

How pleasantly the rising moon,

    Between the shadow of the mows,

    Looked on them through the great elm-boughs!

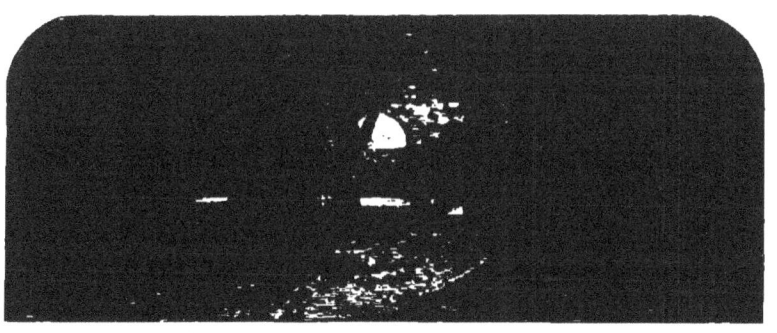

On sturdy boyhood, sun-embrowned,

    On girlhood with its solid curves

    Of healthful strength and painless nerves!

And jests went round, and laughs that made

    The house-dog answer with his howl,

    And kept astir the barn-yard fowl;

Mabel Martin.

And quaint old songs their fathers sung

In Derby dales and Yorkshire moors,

Ere Norman William trod their shores;

And tales, whose merry license shook

The fat sides of the Saxon thane,

Forgetful of the hovering Dane, —

Mabel Martin.

Rude plays to Celt and Cimbri known,

    The charms and riddles that beguiled

    On Oxus' banks the young world's child, —

That primal picture-speech wherein

    Have youth and maid the story told,

    So new in each, so dateless old,

Recalling pastoral Ruth in her

    Who waited, blushing and demure,

    The red-ear's kiss of forfeiture.

PART III

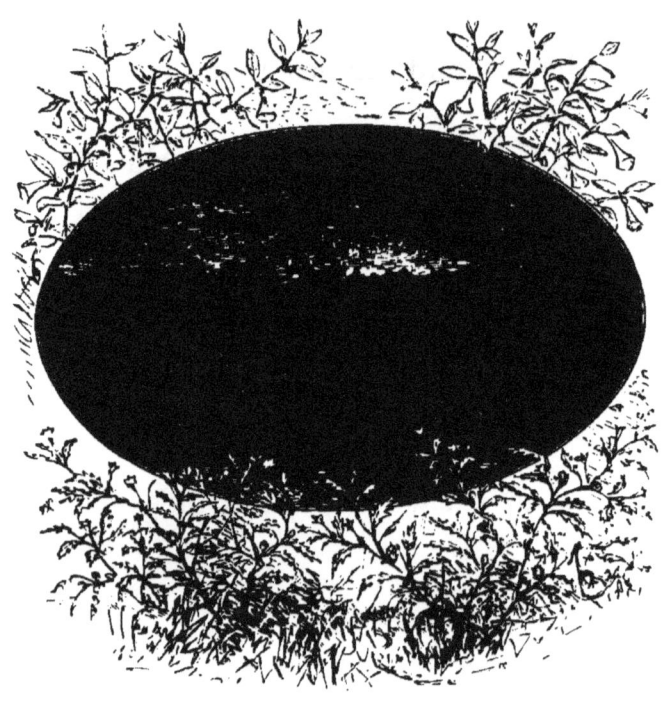

THE WITCH'S DAUGHTER

But still the sweetest voice was mute

That river-valley ever heard

From lips of maid or throat of bird;

For Mabel Martin sat apart,

And let the hay-mow's shadow fall

Upon the loveliest face of all.

Mabel Martin.

She sat apart, as one forbid,

    Who knew that none would condescend

To own the Witch-wife's child a friend.

The seasons scarce had

    gone their round,

Since curious thousands

    thronged to see

Her mother at

    the gallows-tree;

Mabel Martin.

And mocked the prison-palsied limbs

   That faltered on the fatal stairs,

   And wan lip trembling with its prayers!

Few questioned of the sorrowing child,

   Or, when they saw the mother die,

   Dreamed of the daughter's agony.

They went up to their homes that day,

   As men and Christians justified:

   God willed it, and the wretch had died!

Dear God and Father of us all,

   Forgive our faith in cruel lies, —

   Forgive the blindness that denies!

Mabel Martin.

Forgive thy creature when he takes,

    For the all-perfect love thou art,

    Some grim creation of his heart.

Cast down our idols, overturn

    Our bloody altars; let us see

    Thyself in thy humanity!

Young Mabel from her mother's grave

    Crept to her desolate hearth-stone,

    And wrestled with her fate alone;

With love, and anger, and despair,

    The phantoms of disordered sense,

    The awful doubts of Providence!

Mabel Martin.

O, dreary broke the winter days,

And dreary fell the winter nights

When, one by one, the neighboring lights

Mabel Martin.

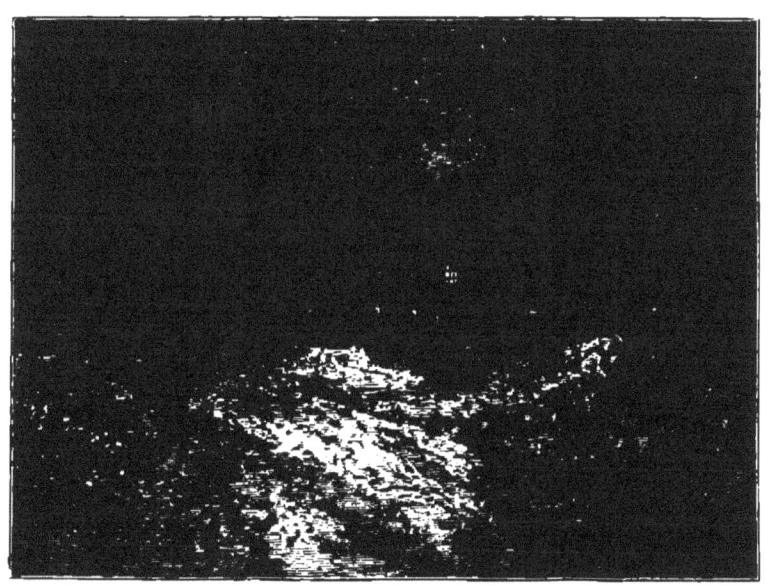

Went out, and human sounds grew still,

And all the phantom-peopled dark

Closed round her hearth-fire's dying spark.

And summer days were sad and long,

And sad the uncompanioned eves,

And sadder sunset-tinted leaves,

Mabel Martin.

And Indian Summer's airs of balm;

    She scarcely felt the soft caress,

    The beauty died of loneliness!

The school-boys jeered her as they passed,

    And, when she sought the house of prayer,

    Her mother's curse pursued her there.

Mabel Martin.

And still o'er many a neighboring door

She saw the horseshoe's curvéd charm,

To guard against her mother's harm:

That mother, poor and sick and lame,

Who daily, by the old arm-chair,

Folded her withered hands in prayer;—

Mabel Martin.

Who turned, in Salem's dreary jail,

Her worn old Bible o'er and o'er,

When her dim eyes could read no more!

Mabel Martin.

Sore tried and pained, the poor girl kept

  Her faith, and trusted that her way,

  So dark, would somewhere meet the day.

And still her weary wheel went round

  Day after day, with no relief:

  Small leisure have the poor for grief.

PART IV

THE CHAMPION

So in the shadow Mabel sits;

    Untouched by mirth she sees and hears,

    Her smile is sadder than her tears.

But cruel eyes have found her out,

    And cruel lips repeat her name,

    And taunt her with her mother's shame.

Mabel Martin.

She answered not with railing words,

    But drew her apron o'er her face,

    And, sobbing, glided from the place.

And only pausing at the door,

    Her sad eyes met the troubled gaze

    Of one who, in her better days,

Mabel Martin.

Had been her warm and steady friend,

Ere yet her mother's doom had made

Even Esek Harden half afraid.

He felt that mute appeal of tears,

And, starting, with an angry frown,

Hushed all the wicked murmurs down.

"Good neighbors mine," he sternly said,

"This passes harmless mirth or jest;

I brook no insult to my guest.

"She is indeed her mother's child;

But God's sweet pity ministers

Unto no whiter soul than hers.

Mabel Martin.

"Let Goody Martin rest in peace;

I never knew her harm a fly,

And witch or not, God knows — not I.

"I know who swore her life away;

And as God lives, I'd not condemn

An Indian dog on word of them."

Mabel Martin.

The broadest lands in all the town,

The skill to guide, the power to awe,

Were Harden's; and his word was law.

None dared withstand him to his face,

But one sly maiden spake aside:

"The little witch is evil-eyed!

Mabel Martin.

"Her mother only killed a cow,

　Or witched a churn or dairy-pan;

　But she, forsooth, must charm a man!"

PART V

IN THE SHADOW

Poor Mabel, homeward turning, passed

The nameless terrors of the wood,

And saw, as if a ghost pursued,

Her shadow gliding in the moon;

The soft breath of the west-wind gave

A chill as from her mother's grave.

Mabel Martin.

How dreary seemed the silent house!
   Wide in the moonbeams' ghastly glare
   Its windows had a dead man's stare!

And, like a gaunt and spectral hand,
   The tremulous shadow of a birch
   Reached out and touched the door's low porch,

As if to lift its latch: hard by,
   A sudden warning call she heard,
   The night-cry of a boding bird.

She leaned against the door; her face,
   So fair, so young, so full of pain,
   White in the moonlight's silver rain.

Mabel Martin.

The river, on its pebbled rim,

Made music such as childhood knew;

The door-yard tree was whispered through

Mabel Martin.

By voices such as childhood's ear

Had heard in moonlights long ago;

And through the willow-boughs below

She saw the rippled waters shine;

Beyond, in waves of shade and light,

The hills rolled off into the night.

Mabel Martin.

She saw and heard, but over all

A sense of some transforming spell,

The shadow of her sick heart fell.

And still across the wooded space

The harvest lights of Harden shone,

And song and jest and laugh went on.

And he, so gentle, true, and strong,

Of men the bravest and the best,

Had he, too, scorned her with the rest?

Mabel Martin.

She strove to drown her sense of wrong,

And, in her old and simple way,

To teach her bitter heart to pray.

Poor child! the prayer, begun in faith,

Grew to a low, despairing cry

Of utter misery: "Let me die!

Mabel Martin.

"Oh! take me from the scornful eyes,

And hide me where the cruel speech

And mocking finger may not reach!

"I dare not breathe my mother's name:

A daughter's right I dare not crave

To weep above her unblest grave!

"Let me not live until my heart,

With few to pity, and with none

To love me, hardens into stone.

"O God! have mercy on thy child,

Whose faith in thee grows weak and small,

And take me ere I lose it all!"

Mabel Martin.

A shadow on the moonlight fell,

And murmuring wind and wave became

A voice whose burden was her name.

PART VI

THE BETROTHAL

HAD then God heard her? Had he sent

His angel down? In flesh and blood,

Before her Esek Harden stood!

He laid his hand upon her arm:

"Dear Mabel, this no more shall be;

Who scoffs at you must scoff at me.

Mabel Martin.

"You know rough Esek Harden well;

And if he seems no suitor gay,

And if his hair is touched with gray,

"The maiden grown shall never find

His heart less warm than when she smiled,

Upon his knees, a little child!"

Mabel Martin.

Her tears of grief were tears of joy,

As, folded in his strong embrace,

She looked in Esek Harden's face.

"O, truest friend of all!" she said,

"God bless you for your kindly thought,

And make me worthy of my lot!"

He led her forth, and, blent in one,

Beside their happy pathway ran

The shadows of the maid and man.

Mabel Martin.

He led her through his dewy fields,

To where the swinging lanterns glowed,

And through the doors the huskers showed.

Mabel Martin.

"Good friends and neighbors!" Esek said,

"I 'm weary of this lonely life;

In Mabel see my chosen wife!

"She greets you kindly, one and all;

The past is past, and all offence

Falls harmless from her innocence.

"Henceforth she stands no more alone;

You know what Esek Harden is; —

He brooks no wrong to him or his.

"Now let the merriest tales be told,

And let the sweetest songs be sung

That ever made the old heart young!

Mabel Martin.

"For now the lost has found a home;

And a lone hearth shall brighter burn,

As all the household joys return!"

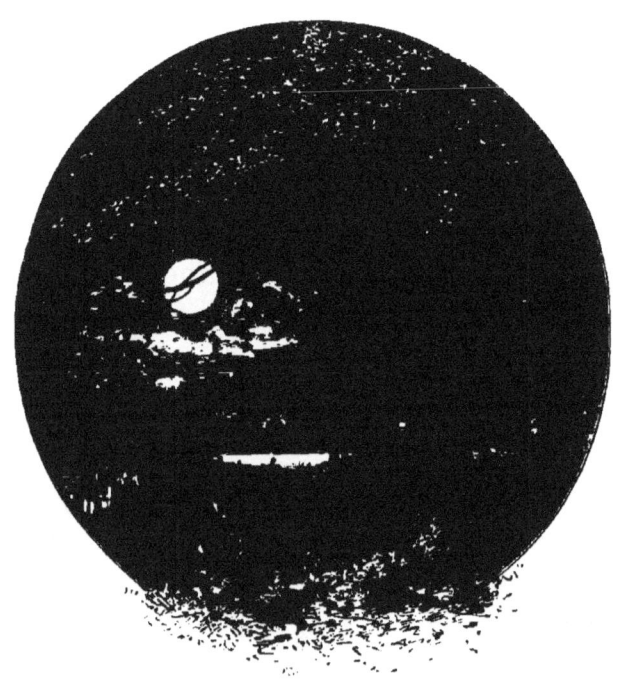

O, pleasantly the harvest-moon,

Between the shadow of the mows,

Looked on them through the great elm-boughs!

Mabel Martin.

On Mabel's curls of golden hair,

On Esek's shaggy strength it fell;

And the wind whispered, "It is well!"

www.ingramcontent.com/pod-product-compliance
Lightning Source LLC
Chambersburg PA
CBHW022152090426
42742CB00010B/1479